"HOW WAS YOUR DAY?"

444 BETTER Questions to Help You Connect with Your Child

Library of Congress Cataloging-in-Publication Data available upon request.

ISBN: 978-1-950500-49-9

duopress books are available at special discounts when purchased in bulk for sales promotions as well as for fund-raising or educational use. Special editions can be created to specification. Contact us at hello@duopressbooks.com for more information.

Manufactured in China

10 9 8 7 6 5 4 3 2 1

Duo Press LLC.
8 Market Place, Suite 300
Baltimore, MD 21202

Distributed by Workman Publishing Company, Inc.
Published simultaneously in Canada by Thomas Allen & Son Limited.

To order: hello@duopressbooks.com

www.duopressbooks.com

www.workman.com

STOP ASKING "HOW WAS YOUR DAY?"

444 BETTER Questions to Help You Connect with Your Child

Daniel J. Crawford

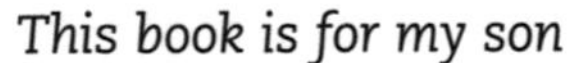

This book is for my son

WELCOME

This book is a tool. It is an introduction to a conversation.

It began as a list of questions taped to the center console of my beat-up 2000 Toyota, a series of curious conversation starters to help my son, his mother, and myself engage in meaningful after-school discussion. He was five years old when I started writing this list, and we had already fallen into an after-school routine that was incomplete and unproductive. There was (and continues to be) a universe of life expanding in the mind and soul of my child, a universe I care about deeply, but at the end of an exhausting day at school, summarizing the entirety of his day in a single moment became a chore.

Something was missing. I recalled the many times in my own life when I had to sum up an experience on the spot, and I remembered just how challenging that can be.

So, I prepared a list of questions in advance.

Over time, I added more, and the list grew longer. I wrote much of this content as a solution for my own family. But the book you have in front of you, I wrote for you, for the parents and caregivers who love their children very much but are struggling to communicate.

How was school?

How was school?

Did you learn anything today?

How was school?

I was asking my son to reduce six hours of his day into a single-syllable reply. And then we would move on. I was reading the headlines but missing the news.

It wasn't his fault. It was mine.

I was asking the wrong questions.

This book helps to find the right ones. Each page presents questions that, in the moment, we don't think to ask. Some of the questions are fun, some are deep and reflective, and some are silly. Some questions will open doors to otherwise difficult conversations about mental health, personality, and identity. Some questions will encourage you to share things you don't otherwise know how to say. The questions are diverse and are appropriate for schoolchildren of all ages and walks of life. They can be asked in any particular order and can be adjusted toward the individual. In addition, this book offers various "Lead by Example" sections—prompts that will encourage you to share with your child something from your own experience.

Human beings crave communication and connection, but we often struggle to find it. These questions bridge that gap.

It is not necessarily the content of the

questions that matters, nor the substance of the replies they elicit. Rather, it is the simple act of communication that carries the greatest weight. Children of all ages will grow to desire some degree of privacy and individuality, and those desires should be respected, of course. This book is not designed as a tool to learn every detail about your child's day. Instead, it is designed to get to know your child as a person, as an individual.

Ultimately, this book is about communication and nothing more. It is comprehensive but demands little time and effort from the parent or caregiver.

In this book, I offer no lectures on parenting. I offer no expertise, no study guides, no lifestyle coaching. I offer only the means to get the ball rolling, to encourage openness, connection, and communication. This book is a tool, to be flipped through while parked in the pick-up line at school, before sitting down to dinner, or anywhere and anytime you please.

Communication is valuable in any relationship, but amid day-to-day stresses and exhausting schedules, it can become a challenge. This book provides solutions. You'll find that these questions lead to more in-depth conversations and stronger relationships. I know there is value in this book, as I have already found it. I encourage you to find it too.

Enjoy.

—Daniel J. Crawford

1

Who sat next to you at lunch today?

2

If you were a **journalist**, what **news topic** would you want to cover?

3

How do you feel when you **meet someone new?** Are you **outgoing** or **reserved?** Do you feel **confident?** **Cautious?**

4

Is there anyone who **tries really hard** but doesn't do well in school?

5

Who is the **most organized** student?

6

Have any of your classmates ever asked **a question that your teacher couldn't answer?**

LEAD BY EXAMPLE

- If I could go back to school, I would study...
- If I could give advice to myself at your age, I would say...
- The most inquisitive person I know is...

7

Do you ever have **trouble concentrating?**

8

Do you think people **act differently** at different times of the day?

9

Would you rather travel to school on a **horse** or in a **hot air balloon**?

10

If we switched places for a week, **how would I do in your classes?** How would you do at **my job?**

11

If you were a phone, how much **battery power** would you have right now?

12

Do you think everything will turn out okay this year?

13

How many **pencils** are in your school?

14

Can you think of a time when you were kind to yourself? Were you **kind to yourself** today?

LEAD BY EXAMPLE

- I'm thankful to my past self for...
- A gift I am giving to my future self is...
- I forgive myself for...
- I am blessed because...

15

Which **subjects** do you wish they taught in school?

16

What's **one song** you wish you could learn to play on any **instrument**?

17

Do you notice people's **eye color**? What about **hair color** or **skin color**?

18

What's the **oldest memory** that you have?

19

If a **famous chef** came to make lunch for your school, what would all the students **want to eat?**

20

Could you make it through an entire day of being **completely silent?**

21

Could everyone in your school go an **entire day** without **speaking?**

22

What was the **funniest thing** that happened today?

23

What makes you **angry** at school?

24

When you get angry, how long does it last and what helps you feel better?

25

Do you ever wait until **the last minute** to finish something?

26

Who inspires you to be better?

LEAD BY EXAMPLE

- One person I really admired as a child was...
- One person I look up to now is...
- When I was a kid, one person who had a big impact on me was...

27

Do you think most **punishments** and **rewards** are effective? If you had to choose your own, **what would you choose?**

28

Is there anyone you **see** every day but have never **spoken** to?

29

Which **teachers** absolutely **love** **what they do**?

30

Would you **learn differently** if you lived in a completely **different country?**

LEAD BY EXAMPLE

- My favorite thing about where we live is...
- My favorite vacation we've been on is...
- One place I've always wanted to visit is...
- A country I've always been fascinated by is...

31

What **catchphrase** is everyone **saying** right now?

32

What is a catchphrase I say that someone **your age** would **never say**?

33

Do you know that it's okay if you're not perfect?

34

What's one thing teachers love but students hate?

35

Why do you think school buses are yellow? **What color would you like your school bus to be?**

36

Do you have **high self-esteem** or **low self-esteem** most of the time?

37

What's the most fun you've had in school?

38

Did you hear a new song that you like this week?

LEAD BY EXAMPLE

- When I was your age, my favorite song was...
- My favorite band was...
- The best concert I've ever been to was...
- One band or musician that I'd like to see in concert is...

39

Do you like **being in class** when it's **raining** outside? What about when it's **sunny**?

40

What is **one thing at school** you are **thankful** for?

41

What **goals** do you have **for school** this year?

42

Have you set any **personal goals** recently? How do you decide what you want to **accomplish**?

43

What is one time you **succeeded** in **accomplishing a goal?** What is one time you **failed** to accomplish a goal?

LEAD BY EXAMPLE

- I want to be remembered for...
- I want people to admire me for...
- Something I'm working on is...
- My long-term goals are...

44

Do you ever feel like you have to **please everyone**?

45

Are there any students who **used to be friends** but aren't friends anymore?

46

What's the **longest word** you know?

47

Do you like to **work alone**, with **one other person**, or with **a group**?

48

If you could **redesign our town or city**, what would you add? What would you take away?

49

If you were **in charge of the class**, how would you **settle an argument** between two students?

50

Do you feel **at home** within yourself?

LEAD BY EXAMPLE

- I am most relaxed when...
- I learned who I really am as a person when...
- I think one of my best qualities is...

51

What is one thing that **other students** are **interested in** that **you aren't?**

52

What is one thing you're interested in that other students aren't?

53

What do you think the **principal** does all day?

54

How much **math** do you think I use on a **daily basis**?

55

What's something **you can teach me** that I don't know?

56

If you started a **charity**, whom or what would you **help**?

57

Was there anything **taught** in school today that **you already knew**?

58

Are you **afraid** of anything?

59

Does anyone at school **chew on their fingernails** or have any other **nervous habits?**

60

What is your **favorite piece** of **art** that you have ever **created**?

61

When do you feel most **productive**?

LEAD BY EXAMPLE

- Today, I woke up thinking about...
- A challenge I faced at work was...
- One thing I'm grateful for today is...
- When I got home, the first thing I wanted to do was...
- Tomorrow, I'm going to prioritize...

62

Is there anyone you have met whom you didn't like at first but grew to like over time?

63

Do you prefer reading **fiction** or **nonfiction**?

64

If you could turn your school into a **mini-golf course**, what **obstacles** would you create and how would you **design** it?

65

If you could **rearrange the alphabet**, what order would you put the letters in?

66

Do you think school is harder for you than it was for me at your age?

67

Has anyone in school discussed how to **manage your time** and **energy**?

68

Is anyone always **drawing** or **doodling** during class?

69

What was your **least favorite part** of the day today?

70

Do your teachers seem to **enjoy what they do?**

71

Which **club** or **team** always seems to be **having the most fun?**

72

What's something **you noticed** today that **no one else noticed?**

73

What kind of **jobs** do you think **other kids** will have when they **finish school**?

LEAD BY EXAMPLE

- The best job I ever had was...
- The hardest job I ever had was...
- My first job was...
- One job I've always wanted to try is...
- The best boss I ever had was...
- My favorite coworker of all time is...
- One thing I learned in school that I use all the time is...

74

Do you like to speak or read to the class?

75

Do you like to **answer questions** when the **teacher asks** the class?

76

Do you ever have trouble finding joy in things?

77

Do you **drink water** during the school day?

78

What's your **favorite** **thing** to **drink** at school **besides water**?

79

What is one thing that surprised you today?

80

How many words do you know?

81

What makes a **book** really fun to **read**?

LEAD BY EXAMPLE

- When I was a kid, I would always ask to hear a story about...
- When I was a kid, I loved to read...
- One of my favorite books that I've read recently is...

82

Who is really emotionally intelligent?

83

Do you prefer learning about your own country or the rest of the world?

84

Did any of your **teachers** go to your **school** when they were **younger**?

85

What's one thing about **your school** that's **unique**?

86

Who is in your friend group?

87

What do you like most about your friends?

88

Is there anything you don't like about your friends?

89

Do you think students are more **motivated** by **rewards** or **punishments**?

LEAD BY EXAMPLE

- Growing up, my chores were...
- One time, I got in a lot of trouble for...
- One time, I was rewarded for...

90

How can you tell if a **poem** is good?

91

Is there **anyone** who seems to be going through a **hard time** right now?

92

If a **newspaper** were published about your life, what would **today's headline** be?

93

How does your class celebrate birthdays?

94

What would be your ideal birthday gift?

95

Do you have **friends** who **bring their lunch** to school? Does anyone come with **food that you wish you could try**?

96

What could you do to **make school better** for students in the future?

97

What is your favorite **smell**?

98

What are you **most proud of** this week?

99

Do you ever feel like **you're doing your best,** but it's not good enough?

LEAD BY EXAMPLE

- The biggest challenge I had today was...
- The best decision I made this week was...
- A big decision I need to make soon is...
- If I get discouraged, I feel better when...

100

If your school had a **parade**, what type of **float** would you **create**?

101

Who **walks the fastest** in your school?

102

Do any of your **teachers** have **children**?

103

If you could bring **one musician** to your school to play a **concert**, whom would you ask?

104

Do you think **students 1,000 years ago** felt the same way about education that you do?

105

Which **class** is the **most fun**?

106

Do you **trust people** right when you meet them or do you have to get to know them first?

107

Is it hard or easy to **earn** your trust?

108

What **movies** do kids like to **quote**?

109

Is there anyone who **always talks** but **doesn't listen**?

110

Do you have **a strong sense of identity?**

111

Does your **school** do a good job of helping students discover **who they are?**

112

What **time** of **day** do you feel at your **best**?

LEAD BY EXAMPLE

- My favorite month is...
- My favorite day of the year is...
- My favorite season is...
- My favorite year of my life, so far, is...
- My favorite holiday is...
- One event I wish I could attend again is...

113

Would you rather take a class on **how to cook meals** or on **how to bake desserts?**

114

What's one **brave thing** you've done recently?

115

What **period of history** would you **travel** to if you could?

116

Is there anyone in your class who always seems **really happy?**

LEAD BY EXAMPLE

- One thing that makes me happy is...
- Something I have learned about happiness is...
- A person I know who always looks on the bright side is...

117

What are the **most comfortable clothes** you own?

118

What's something that **challenged you** today?

119

What kind of **math** are you **best** at?

120

Do you ever have **conversations** with other people **in your head** after the conversation has **already happened**?

121

Is there **anyone** at school you would like to **get to know better?**

122

Did you have a hard time **motivating yourself** to do something today? What was it?

123

Can you think of a **situation** where you **motivated yourself**? What did you do?

LEAD BY EXAMPLE

- Something that has been on my to-do list for a long time is...
- One of my favorite motivational quotes is...
- The most inspiring person I have ever met is...
- If I could meet one of my personal heroes, I would choose...

124

How many **doors** does your **school** have?

125

Which **teacher** or **staff** member has **the hardest job?**

126

Should there be more education about **money** and **finances**?

127

Are there any **twins** in school? Do they look alike or different?

128

Has someone ever **given their word** and then gone back on it?

129

What did you **do well** today?

130

Would your classes be more interesting if you met more **people** who actually used your **school subjects** in **day-to-day life**?

131

Did anything or anyone **hurt your** feelings today?

132

What **food** cheers you up at lunch?

133

Have you ever had a **hard time admitting** you made **a mistake**?

134

What makes you **empathize** with a person?

135

What **vocabulary word** have you learned most recently?

136

How **quickly** could you learn a **foreign language**?

137

What's one thing your school **does really well?**

138

Do you think your environment at school is one of **healthy stress** or **unhealthy stress?**

LEAD BY EXAMPLE

- Lately, I have been stressed out by...
- One way I deal with stressful feelings is...
- To try to manage stress I usually...

139

Do you ever feel **exhausted**? What's the **longest** stretch of time that you've felt this way?

140

If your school had one week to **break a world record**, what record would you want to break?

141

What **song** is everyone **obsessed** with right now?

142

If you were stranded on a **deserted island** and could bring only **one textbook**, which book would you choose?

143

Have you ever noticed a **rumor** spreading through your school?

144

What **grades** would you give each of your **teachers**?

145

Does anyone seem different from the person they were last year?

146

What is your favorite outfit?

LEAD BY EXAMPLE

- When I was a kid, my favorite hat was...
- My favorite shoes were...
- My favorite accessory was...
- I played dress-up with...
- My grandparents or other family members wore...
- My parents or guardians wore...
- My siblings or friends wore...

147

Are there kids who always try to **break** the rules?

148

Do your **emotions** ever have an impact on **how** you **behave**?

149

If your school gave you more of a say in **what and how you are taught,** what would you change?

150

What's the **best thing that could happen** during a random school day?

151

Who has the **loudest voice** in school?

152

What kind of **paintings** do you like?

153

Have you ever been **blamed** for **something** you **didn't do?**

154

Is there **someone** you **trust** at school?

155

If you could **vote** to change **one thing** about your school, what would you vote for? What would **other kids** vote for?

156

If you had to come up with **one question** that **only I** would know the answer to, what question would it be?

157

Are there students who are always **really quiet?**

158

What's **the most exciting thing** that happened today?

159

Do you ever have **a hard time** trying your best?

160

If your school had one room that possessed **magical powers**, where would it be located? **What kind** of magical powers would it have? **Who** would know about it?

LEAD BY EXAMPLE

- The biggest house I have ever been in is...
- When I grew up, the house I lived in was...
- Growing up, I wondered what it would be like if I lived in...

161

Who was in a **bad mood** today?

162

Which **teacher** has the **most patience**?

163

If you made **a documentary about your school**, what would you call it? What would you want to **feature**? Whom would you **interview**?

164

Have you ever **forgotten someone's name** right after you heard it?

165

When were you the most **bored** you've ever been in **class**?

166

If you started a company, which students or teachers at your school would you want to **work** for you?

167

What's your favorite candy?

168

What's something you **think** about that adults **never talk about?**

169

Do you prefer to be in the company of **other people** or **by yourself?**

170

Is it important to have **alone time?**

171

Whom does everyone **respect**?

172

Should schools teach **how to have a healthy argument** or conflict?

173

What do you think life was like **before** people had **refrigerators**?

174

Which classroom has the most interesting **stuff on the walls**?

175

Do you have a **favorite tree?**

176

Is there anyone who **seems** **really sad?**

LEAD BY EXAMPLE

- One thing that makes me sad is...
- One thing I do when I feel sad is...
- One thing I do when I notice someone else is sad is...

177

Are kids **smarter** today than they were **a hundred years ago?**

178

Where do you sit in class?

179

What makes your day go by really quickly?

180

If your history class **had a pet**, what would its **name** be?

181

If you could **study abroad** anywhere in the **world**, where would you go?

182

Who is **the tallest person** in your school?

183

Do you ever **drift off** when someone else is **talking**?

184

What is one thing you **succeeded** at today? What is one thing you **failed** at?

185

What kind of **future** do you want to **create** for yourself?

LEAD BY EXAMPLE

- I am becoming...
- I am most productive when...
- When I was a kid, I imagined that I would grow up to be...

186

What's something at your school that **never seems to be working?**

187

Have you noticed whether **certain foods** affect your **mood**?

188

Do you notice what affects your **energy level?**

LEAD BY EXAMPLE

- For breakfast today, I ate...
- A routine or a food that usually gets me going in the morning is...
- For lunch today, I ate...
- My favorite midday snack is...
- Here is what makes me feel great after lunch...
- I eat lunch in different places sometimes. Today, that place was...
- Sometimes I get myself a treat during the day, such as...

189

Is there **anyone** at school you wish you could **spend more time** with?

190

What's one thing you've been meaning to do that you haven't gotten around to?

191

Do you like classes **where you have to think** to figure out the answers or classes where you have to **memorize the answers** and then recall them?

192

What's the **weirdest word** you've learned?

193

Can any of the **students** at your school **speak another language?**

194

Should **adults** have to go **back to school** to relearn all the things they forgot?

195

Have you had more **good days** or **bad days** this month?

196

Are you ever really **hard on yourself**, even if it's just **internally**?

197

Do you think **other kids struggle** with some of the same things you do **mentally, physically,** or **emotionally**?

198

How many **books** are in your school?

199

Do the **seats at school** help students to have correct **posture**?

200

What is the **hardest job** in the **world**?

201

What is the **most rewarding** job in the **world**?

202

What is a **sport** that is not part of most schools' **athletic programs** but should be?

203

Do you ever **dream** about **school**?

LEAD BY EXAMPLE

- One dream I still remember is...
- Recently, my dreams have been...
- I think that dreams tell you...

204

What **challenges** do you **enjoy** taking on? What challenges do you **dread** facing?

205

If your school **suddenly got $100,000**, what would they use it for?

206

What would you do if you suddenly became **invisible** during school?

207

What makes you **feel loved**?

208

Is there anything you need **my help** or **support** with?

209

What TV **shows** are all the students **talking** about right now?

210

How would a stranger describe your personality after meeting you for five minutes? What about after five months?

211

How would a **friend** describe your personality?

212

What **life skills** should be taught in school?

213

What kind of **books** do your teachers have on their **desks** or on their **bookshelves**?

LEAD BY EXAMPLE

- The last book I read was...
- An article I read this week was...
- The last movie I watched was...
- A video I enjoyed watching was...
- The last activity I enjoyed was...

214

Are the **computers** at your school **fast** or **slow**?

215

What was the **most frustrating thing** that happened today?

216

Does this year seem harder than last year?

217

If you taught a class, what **subject** would you **teach**?

218

Which **day** of the school week are people **most engaged?**

219

If you could go back in time to the beginning of this week, what would you **tell yourself**? What about the beginning of the month? The school **year**?

220

What's something **romantic** someone has done at school?

221

What is the **earliest** you've ever had to **wake up**?

222

What helps you **rest** when your mind is **exhausted**?

223

Do you think your school has a lot of **money** or has to be **careful** with its **budget**?

LEAD BY EXAMPLE

- As an adult, the longest I've gone without spending money was...
- One thing I have learned about money is...
- The best purchase I ever made was...
- When I was a kid, I wanted to save up my money for...

224

Which of your classmates comes from the **biggest family?**

225

Has there ever been a time when you wished someone would have **stuck up for you?**

226

How could your **school** be better at **recycling**?

227

What was the **most impactful moment** in **human history**?

228

If you had to **name the hallways of your school,** what names would you choose?

229

Are some people more **naturally gifted** at certain subjects?

230

Have any of your **teachers** ever been **wrong** about anything?

231

Was anyone having a **bad day** today?

232

What is one thing that you find **distracting** at school?

233

What is the **best way** to **learn something**? Have you experimented with different **learning styles**?

234

Who **arrives** at the school **first** in the morning?

235

Have you noticed any **strange coincidences** recently?

236

Which **teacher** has the **worst handwriting?** Which **student** has the worst handwriting?

237

What is your favorite **dessert**?

238

What **book** would be most useful to have if you were lost in the **wilderness**? What **tool** would be most useful to have?

239

What **country** or **culture** do you want to learn more about?

240

Do any of your **teachers** have a **quote or saying** that they use all the time?

241

Do any of your classmates have **pets**?

242

What **brightens** up your **day** at school?

243

How often **do** you **feel sad** at school?

244

How many **beach balls** do you think you could fit into your school?

245

Did you apologize to **anyone** today?

246

Have you ever felt like you **shouldn't** have had to **apologize** for something?

LEAD BY EXAMPLE

- One time I should have said sorry was...
- One lie that I regret telling is...
- When I was young, I got in trouble for...
- The best apology that I ever received was...

247

Is there anyone who seems to **worry too much** about schoolwork?

248

Who seems like they need **more sleep**?

249

Do you have someone your age that **you can talk to about anything?** What about a **grown-up?**

250

Before you speak up in class, do you **rehearse** what you are going to **say**?

LEAD BY EXAMPLE

- Something I am really self-conscious about is...
- The best speech I ever heard was...
- If I have to speak in front of people, I prepare by...

251

Is there anyone who already knows **what they want to do with their life?**

252

What's something you have **learned** that **most adults** don't know?

253

Would you go to school **six days a week** if it gave you a **longer summer break?**

254

If your **teachers** were in a band, what would the **band's name** be?

255

Do you **wish** you had **more friends?**

256

Is there **someone** you are thinking of **befriending?**

LEAD BY EXAMPLE

- One thing I have learned about friendship is...
- When I was your age, my best friend was...
- One time I felt like I didn't have many friends was...

257

Do you have any **hopes** or **dreams** that **you just can't shake?**

258

Do you ever feel **hopeless?**

LEAD BY EXAMPLE

- I think it's really brave that...
- One time I almost gave up was...
- If I'm feeling down, I try to cheer myself up by...

259

What **games** do the other **kids** at your school like to **play**?

260

What classes won't be necessary to teach in the future?

261

If you could go on a **field trip anywhere in the world**, where would you go?

LEAD BY EXAMPLE

- The longest road trip I've ever been on was...
- When I was a kid, these were the games I liked to play in the car...
- My favorite state park or field trip was...

262

What do you think **your school** spends the **most money** on?

263

Who is the **best** at saying "**please**" and "**thank you**"?

264

Who is the best at **sharing**?

265

Have you ever felt like **people think** you are **weird**? Do you think **other kids** feel that way sometimes? What about **grown-ups**?

266

When was the last time **someone gave you a compliment?** What was it?

267

What was one point today when **life was good?**

268

Which **student** never wants any **help**?

269

Is there anyone who seems really **responsible** for their **age**?

270

What would you do if you woke up **tomorrow morning** and it was **today** again?

271

What's one **recipe** you wish you knew **how to make**?

272

Do you think school is **harder** or **easier** than it was **hundreds of years ago**?

273

Would students be more **interested** if they got to **choose** what **books to read** for a class?

LEAD BY EXAMPLE

- My favorite book that I had to read for school was...
- My favorite teacher was...
- My favorite subject was...
- A subject I wish I had learned more about was...
- I once did a research project on...

274

What do you think is the **best job** for someone **your age**?

275

Is there a **class** that you just **don't enjoy**?

276

Have you ever **pretended not to know** something that you actually did know?

277

Have you **pretended to know** something you didn't know?

278

Would you **learn more or less** if your school had **couches** instead of **chairs**?

279

Who has an **odd talent?**

280

Is there anyone who is **really competitive** in your class?

281

Do you prefer learning about **ancient history** or would you rather study **modern history?**

282

How long would it take you to write a book?

283

Do you ever think about **life and death?**

LEAD BY EXAMPLE

- One thing I am afraid of is...
- One thing I used to be afraid of is...
- I overcame my fear when...

284

If you could time-travel, what would you say to an **earlier version of yourself?**

285

If a **future version** of you **time-traveled** back to this moment, what do you think Future You would have to say?

286

Who is the **kindest student** at school?

287

What's the **latest** you've ever **gone to sleep**?

288

If you had to design the **perfect school bus**, what would it be like?

289

Do you ever feel **peer pressure**?

290

Was there ever anything that turned out not to be **as hard as you thought** it would be?

291

Who at your school has the **most school spirit**?

292

Are any of the **teachers** really **bad with technology**?

293

If your school offered a **class** in the middle of the night where you could study **stars and planets** through giant **telescopes**, would you sign up?

294

What do you **admire** about yourself?

295

What's one thing **other people admire** about you?

296

Is there anyone who really **struggles with math?**

297

What kind of **tables** are in the **lunchroom** at your school?

298

If you had to describe your **teachers** using the name of a **TV show or movie**, what would you choose?

LEAD BY EXAMPLE

- When I was your age, my favorite movie was...
- The first movie I watched in the theater was...
- My first album (CD, tape, record) was...
- The first concert I ever went to was...
- When I was your age, my favorite book was...

299

If you taught **history**, what could you do to make it really **exciting**?

300

Did anyone have an **argument** today?

301

Do you ever feel **disconnected** from **other people?**

LEAD BY EXAMPLE

- One thing I really miss is...
- One person I wish I could see more often is...
- Someone I lost touch with and would like to reconnect with is...
- When I want to feel connected to other people, I usually...

302

If you had to bring an **afternoon snack** for the **whole school**, what would you bring?

303

Is there a student that you know has a **good heart** but **doesn't show** it?

304

Are there any **words** that you have only said out loud **one time in your life?**

305

What **drains** **you** of energy?

306

Do you believe that **people** are **generally** **good**?

307

Have you ever felt like you knew the **answer** to a question that a teacher asked but **were afraid to say it?**

308

What would a **class about happiness** be like?

309

Would your **classes** be better if there were **fewer students**?

310

Do you have a **favorite pen** or **pencil**?

311

If you could **paint** your school **any color**, what color would it be?

312 Who is the **most** **active** student?

313 Who loves to **learn new things?**

314

What was your **favorite thing** that happened today?

315

Do you think one person can change the world?

316

Do you ever feel **lonely** or **empty**?

317

Do you **believe in yourself**?

LEAD BY EXAMPLE

- I have self-worth because...
- One thing I failed at when I was younger was...
- One thing I never gave up on was...

318

If you could **create anything** you wanted in **art class**, with unlimited time and resources, what would you make?

319

Do you like the **layout** of your **school**?

320

Is there **anyone** who can always **make you laugh?**

321

Is there anyone who is always **mean?**

LEAD BY EXAMPLE

- The most I've ever laughed was...
- The last time I cried was...
- One time my face hurt from smiling was...

322

What's **something** interesting you heard today?

323

Do you have a **favorite** **drinking fountain?**

324

What could your school do to promote a **healthier lifestyle**?

325

Do your **teachers** explain why you should learn the **subjects** they teach?

326

Do you think the **world** **outside** your school is generally **fair** or **unfair**?

327

Has anything **happened** in your **classroom** that you thought was **unfair**?

328

Do you think your **teachers** are **fair**?

329

Is there **anything coming up** that you are **dreading**?

330

Is there anything coming up that you're **excited** for?

LEAD BY EXAMPLE

- My best memory of school is...
- My worst memory of school is...
- My best memory as an adult is...
- One of my oldest memories is...

331

Do you **work better** when you have a **deadline** or when you have **unlimited time?**

332

If you had to take a **knitting class**, what would you knit?

333

Is there **anyone** at school who makes you feel **envious**?

334

If you could call **anyone** in the world to **ask about their day**, whom would you call?

335

What makes you **sad**?

336

What **emotional strength** have you had at school this week?

337

Who is the **least organized teacher**?

338

Would you rather have a **school-wide game of tag** or **hide-and-seek**?

339

What would **college** and **adult recess** be like?

LEAD BY EXAMPLE

- One thing I miss about being a kid is...
- When your grandparents' generation was young, they...
- When I was a kid, the most popular activities at recess were...
- At my school, lunch was usually...

340

What is the **longest book** you have read?

341

If you could travel to **any historical site**, where would you go?

342

What's one **food** you've always been **afraid to try?**

343

What's one food you've always **wanted to try?**

344

Can you think of a food that **you didn't think you would like**, but when you tried it, you loved it?

LEAD BY EXAMPLE

- The best dinner I ever had was...
- When I was a kid, I loved to eat...
- When I was a kid, I hated eating...
- One food we'd always have on holidays was...
- The weirdest food I've ever tried is...
- A food I didn't like as a kid that I love to eat now is...
- Growing up, I ate a lot of...

345

If you had to **design a school uniform**, what would it look like?

346

Should **students** still learn how to **farm** and grow **crops**?

347

Do you think you are **kind to others?**

348

Have you ever noticed someone **taking advantage** of your **kindness** or **generosity?**

349

In which **class** do you **look at the clock** the most?

LEAD BY EXAMPLE

- When I was a kid, I liked to play...
- The last time I climbed a tree was...
- The last time I ran through a sprinkler was...
- The last time I flew a kite was...

350

Would you travel to **outer space** if it meant you had to live on a **tiny ship** for a year?

351

Does your **school** have a **distinctive smell**?

352

If you could be **pen pals** with a student from anywhere in the world, what **city** or **country** would you pick?

353

Do you like to study subjects that are **subjective** or **objective**?

354

Is it okay to **question everything**?

355

Which **students** are really **outgoing**?

356

Is there **anyone** who always seems **optimistic**?

357

Are there certain **walls** or **doors** that you **touch** every time you **walk past** them?

LEAD BY EXAMPLE

- The farthest I've ever walked is...
- My favorite building is...
- One little superstition I have is...

358

What do your **teachers** get really **excited** about?

359

What is the **most popular donut flavor?**

360

Would you rather go to school in a **castle** or on a **giant ship?**

361

What is your **favorite instrument** to hear?

362

Is there anything you wish we talked about more?

LEAD BY EXAMPLE

- I feel confident when...
- I feel proud when...
- I feel accepted when...
- I feel loved when...

363

Did you receive any **criticism** today?

364

What's the most **memorable conversation** you've had at school?

365

Is there anyone at school who has really **low self-esteem?**

366

What's the most **comfortable seat** in all of your **classrooms?**

367

Which **teacher** has the most interesting **life story?**

368

Would most **adults** be able to **pass any of the tests** you have to take?

369

If you could build a tiny model of **any building**, **structure**, or **landscape** in the world, what would you create?

370

Is there anything you've been **afraid** to **talk to me** about?

371

Do you know that **you can always come to me** if you are feeling hopeless, no matter what?

372

What do you think the **very first school** was like?

373

What makes **time** go by really **quickly**?

374

Do you ever have days when **you like the way** you **look**, and days **when** you **don't**?

375

Is there **anyone at school** who always seems to be **sick**?

376

Who has the most unique hobby?

377

What is your favorite mode of transportation?

LEAD BY EXAMPLE

- A hobby I wish I did more often is...
- My favorite board game is...
- My favorite outdoor game or sport is...
- One hobby that I plan to take up is...
- One thing I would love to do but am not very good at is...

378

In what ways could your **school** be **less wasteful**?

379

Do you prefer to read **old works of fiction** or **newer ones**?

380

Which **teacher** has the hardest time **enforcing the rules**?

381

If you could skip school and **go anywhere for a day**, where would you want to go?

382

What would a **class** about **mental health** be like?

383

How can you tell if someone is in **trouble**?

384

Can you tell me about a **decision** you had to make **recently**?

385

Is it easier for you to **make decisions right away** or to **wait?**

386

Would you rather **your life's work** showed up in the future in a **history textbook** or an **art museum**?

387

What is the **best present** you've ever received?

LEAD BY EXAMPLE

- When I was a kid, my bedroom looked like...
- One of my prized possessions was...
- As a kid, I cleaned my room once a (day, week, month)...

388

If you could **bring a pet to school**, what would you bring?

389

What **class** does everyone **pay attention** in?

390

What is the **oldest book** you have read?

391

If your class could **conduct any science experiment**—with unlimited funds and no injuries—what experiment would you choose?

392

What **pizza topping** have you never tried?

393

Would you rather take a **creative writing class** or a **journalism class**?

394

Have you ever had a **great idea** for an **invention**?

395

Would it be difficult for you to **speak** in front of a group or **teach** a class for **an entire day**?

LEAD BY EXAMPLE

- The largest group of people I have ever spoken to is...
- The most nervous I have ever been was...
- Tricks I use to calm myself down are...

396

Do you feel **confident** today?

397

Who at school **talks about themselves** a lot?

398

Has anyone you know been to **another country?**

399

What would your **classes** have been like **one hundred years ago?**

LEAD BY EXAMPLE

- Five years ago, I was probably...
- One year ago today, I was probably...
- One month ago, I was probably...
- One week ago, I was probably...

400

What makes you feel **social anxiety?**

401

What **language** do you wish you knew how to **speak?**

402

Do you have any **teachers** that always seem to be in a **good mood**?

403

What's the **strangest book** you have read?

404

Who asks the most questions in class?

405

What's your favorite classroom?

LEAD BY EXAMPLE

- For me, the most peaceful place to work is...
- When I was in school, my favorite place to be was...
- As a kid, I wished I could spend more time at...

406

What **club** or **team** do you wish your school had?

407

If you could change your **school mascot** to anything, what would it be?

408

If your school had a **zoo** with animals that the students cared for, what **animals** would you choose to have?

409

Do you feel that you are able to **set strong boundaries**?

410

Who has the **longest hair** in school?

411

What is **one** **mistake** that you made today?

412

What do you do **when you make a mistake?**

413

Did anything bring you joy today?

LEAD BY EXAMPLE

- One thing I am at peace with is...
- One thing that bothers me is...
- I am going to choose to be happy about...

414

Do you think schools should teach more about **food** and **eating**?

415

Would you rather **try something new** that you might not be good at or **keep doing what you have already learned** to do well?

416

If your **school** got to create a **national holiday**, what would it be?

417

What are all the students **obsessed with** right now?

418

Does **anyone** in **your class** seem like a **picky eater**?

419

Does anyone eat the **same food** every day?

420

What do your **teachers** do when they **aren't in school?**

421

Are you ever **afraid of rejection?**

LEAD BY EXAMPLE

- The hardest I have ever worked was...
- A project I'm really proud of is...
- A future project I'd like to tackle is...

422

Does your school do a good job teaching **social skills** and **interaction**?

423

If someone painted a **portrait of you**, what would you want to be **wearing**?

LEAD BY EXAMPLE

- One shirt I wish I still had is...
- One outfit I loved as a kid that is no longer in style was...
- A style kids are wearing now that I really like is...

424

What's one **drink** you've always wanted to **try**?

425

If your school got to pick a **restaurant or chef** to make lunch for the students, whom would everyone **vote** for?

426

Who in your school said the **most words** today?

427

What do you think is **important to learn** in school?

LEAD BY EXAMPLE

- When I was a kid, my desk looked like...
- When I got home from school, I used to...
- My favorite place to do homework was...
- The class that gave me the most homework was...
- After finishing my homework, I would often...

428

Would you rather go to school for a day on a **train** or on a **ferry boat**?

429

If the students got to choose a **positive slogan** for the school, what would it be?

430

Are there any **students** who **don't seem to get a subject?**

431

Do you think you ever **crossed paths** with any of your **friends** before you officially met them?

432

Should schools teach **psychology**?

433

If you **wrote a book**, what would it be about?

434

Has anyone ever thought you were **doing something wrong** when you weren't?

435

Did you see anyone **show empathy** today?

436

If you got to write the **headline story** for the school **newspaper**, what would you write about?

437

Do you ever have **racing thoughts**?

LEAD BY EXAMPLE

- When I go to sleep at night, I like to think about...
- I sleep really well when...
- When I wake up in the morning, I...

438

Did anyone have a **birthday** today?

439

How long would it take you to run all the way **around the outside** of your school?

440

What do you think the teachers **talk** about in the **teachers' lounge**?

441

If you could throw a party that is historically themed, what **era**, **decade**, or **historical moment** would you choose?

442

What's the **happiest** day you've had at school **this year**?

443

Would you like to hear about my **day**?

LEAD BY EXAMPLE

- On the day you were born,
  I remember...

444

Do you know that I love you?